Enneagram 6: The Loyalist

Personal Development Strategies for Enneagram Type 6

MATTHEW BRIGHTHOUSE

recipient reader. Under no circumstances will any legal responsibility or blame be held against the publisher for any reparation, damages, or monetary loss due to the information herein, either directly or indirectly.

Respective authors own all copyrights not held by the publisher.

The information herein is offered for informational purposes solely and is universal as so. The presentation of the information is without contract or any type of guarantee assurance.

The trademarks that are used are without any consent, and the publication of the trademark is without permission or backing by the trademark owner. All trademarks and brands within this book are for clarifying purposes only and are owned by the owners themselves, not affiliated with this document.

Contents

Introduction

As an Enneagram 6, it's important to remember that your personality type doesn't define you. It's not set in stone, and you have the ability to learn new ways of being and doing. As you read about your type, some aspects may resonate with you while others may not. Take what works for you and leave the rest.

Like all Enneagram types, 6s have both strengths and blind spots. Your patterns are not inherently good or bad, but have served you in different ways throughout your life. By examining these patterns, you can determine which ones align with your goals and which ones do not - and how your instincts manifest when you're healthy versus when you're stressed.

It's important to remember that personality is fluid. Being an Enneagram 6 does not mean that you always act like a 6, nor should you define yourself solely by this type. Consider it as a spectrum where you can move the pin back and forth to find the sweet spot that works best for you.

At present, your subconscious likely has most of the

control. But by learning about yourself and becoming more conscious, you can lead a more fulfilling and aligned life. And remember, there is no deadline to this process - take it at your own pace.

Lastly, remember that you are a unique individual with a story all your own. Your personality does not define you, and no two people of the same type will be exactly the same. The stories shared in this book are meant to serve as a reference point for understanding the typical tendencies of Enneagram 6s.

Bonus Download

We will examine each area of life in detail for practical tips to help you improve it in the ensuing chapters. The wheel of life technique will be the foundation for this. Fortunately, a life coach has made the worksheet and video walkthrough for this process available for free download. It is recommended that you begin the exercise at the beginning of this book, or at the very least before you read the section on strategy, so that you can accurately assess your current situation in each area of your life.

Your ongoing self-development work will be based on this.

The gift is available here.

https://intralifestyle.com/wol-gift/

An Enneagram 6 Story

As she sat at her desk, Sarah felt her anxiety begin to rise. She had just been given a new project at work and was already feeling overwhelmed. As a type 6, Sarah was reliable, hard-working, and responsible, which often led to her being given more responsibilities than her colleagues. While she enjoyed being recognized for her capabilities, it also caused her to feel an immense pressure to perform at her best, which could sometimes become overwhelming.

Sarah knew that she was an excellent troubleshooter and could foresee problems before they occurred, which is why she was often called upon to take charge of difficult situations. However, this also meant that she was always running on stress, even though she complained about it. Her colleagues and friends often joked about her being a "worrywart," but Sarah knew that her anxiety was simply a part of who she was.

As she stared at the blank screen in front of her, Sarah felt a wave of panic wash over her. She couldn't seem to focus on the task at hand, and her mind was racing with all the possible scenarios that could go wrong with the project. She began to second-guess herself and wondered if she was the right person for the job.

Sarah was cautious by nature and tended to be indecisive when it came to making big decisions. She often found herself seeking validation and reassurance from others before taking action. This caused her to become even more anxious as she waited for their responses, which could sometimes take longer than she would like.

However, Sarah was also reactive, defiant, and rebellious when she felt like her values were being threatened. She had a strong sense of justice and would not hesitate to speak up if she felt like something was unfair. This had led to her standing up for her colleagues many times, even if it meant going against her superiors.

After taking a few deep breaths, Sarah realized that she needed to focus on the task at hand and not let her anxiety get the best of her. She began to break down the project into smaller, more manageable tasks, which made it easier for her to focus. She also reached out to her colleagues for help and advice, which gave her the reassurance she needed to move forward.

As the days went by, Sarah found that she was making progress on the project, and her anxiety began to dissipate. She realized that her strength as a type 6 lay in her ability to foresee problems and foster cooperation. She was able to bring her team together and work towards a common goal, which ultimately led to the success of the project.

Looking back on the experience, Sarah realized that her anxiety and indecisiveness were not weaknesses but rather part of what made her an excellent troubleshooter. By acknowledging her strengths and leaning into them, Sarah was able to overcome her anxiety and achieve her goals.

From that day forward, Sarah continued to be a reliable, hard-working, and responsible employee, but she also learned to embrace her reactive, defiant, and rebellious side when it came to standing up for her values. She knew that her type 6 personality had its strengths and weaknesses, but by accepting who she was, she was able to thrive in both her personal and professional life.

What is an Enneagram 6?

The path to healing and self-discovery is not always easy, but for those who dare to embark on the journey, the rewards are immeasurable. As an Enneagram Type 6, you may feel a constant need for security and safety, but understanding your patterns and behaviors can help you overcome your fears and live a more fulfilling life.

The Enneagram is a valuable tool for gaining self-knowledge, and it has been used for over a century to understand different personality types. Type 6 falls under the Mind center triad, which means that their personalities are built around their thinking patterns and the way they process information. This triad includes Types 5, 6, and 7, and each has a unique way of dealing with stress and emotions.

Type 6 personalities tend to feel anxious and insecure, and they seek out safety and security in their lives. They are often loyal and dependable, but they may also struggle with indecisiveness and self-doubt. Understanding your Enneagram Type can help you gain insight into your patterns of behavior and how they affect your relationships and your overall well-being.

One important aspect of the Enneagram is the concept of wings. Your Enneagram Type is not set in stone, and you can exhibit traits of neighboring Types as well. As a Type 6, you may have a 5 wing or a 7 wing, each of which brings a unique set of characteristics to your personality.

For example, if you have a 6w5 personality, you may be more analytical and introverted, and you may seek out knowledge and information to feel more secure. On the other hand, if you have a 6w7 personality, you may be more outgoing and adventurous, and you may seek out new experiences to combat your fears and anxieties. We'll get into this in more detail later on.

Understanding your patterns of behavior at different levels of stress is also key to gaining self-knowledge. As a Type 6, you may exhibit different behaviors depending on your level of stress. At low levels of stress, you may be loyal, supportive, and responsible. However, at high levels of stress, you may become paranoid, anxious, and fearful.

For example, let's say you're a Type 6 and you're at work. You're given a project to complete, and you start to feel anxious about making a mistake. As the deadline approaches, your anxiety increases, and you start to doubt yourself and your abilities. You may become indecisive, second-guessing your decisions, and seeking reassurance from others.

In this scenario, your Enneagram Type 6 is exhibiting behaviors associated with high levels of stress. However, by understanding your patterns of behavior and how they affect you, you can learn to manage your anxiety and make more confident decisions.

The Enneagram is a powerful tool for gaining self-knowledge and understanding your patterns of behavior. As an Enneagram Type 6, you may struggle with anxiety and insecurity, but by understanding your personality and the behaviors associated with it, you can learn to overcome your fears and live a more fulfilling life. Remember, knowledge is power, and by taking control of your thoughts and behaviors, you can build more authentic relationships, align your life with your values, and improve your overall well-being.

Enneagram Six Main Characteristics

What is it like to be a Six?

Generally, Six is referred to as the Loyalist, known for their love for security and fear of uncertainty. Another word associated with this personality type, that is not as positive, is skeptic. That is quite generic, so how does it translate to everyday behavior and patterns?

You are a Six if you have consistently:

Felt anxious about the future and the potential negative outcomes. You may find yourself seeking reassurance from others and being hesitant to make decisions on your own. You may also struggle with overthinking and analyzing situations to anticipate potential problems.

Experienced fear or unease in situations where you feel unsupported or alone. You may seek out groups or communities to belong to and may struggle with feeling like an outsider. You may also place a high value on loyalty and dependability in relationships.

Felt a strong sense of responsibility to others and to society. You may feel like it is your duty to be a responsible citizen and to do your part to make the world a better place. You may also feel a strong sense of duty to protect and care for those close to you.

Struggled with self-doubt and uncertainty. You may be hesitant to trust your own instincts and may seek out the advice and opinions of others before making decisions. You may also struggle with feeling like you are not good enough or capable enough.

Felt a need for structure and routine. You may feel more comfortable in environments where there are clear rules and expectations, and where you know what is expected of you. You may also struggle with adapting to change or uncertainty.

Experienced a sense of loyalty to authority figures or institutions. You may place a high value on following rules and regulations, and may struggle with questioning authority or going against the status quo. You may also feel a sense of duty to protect and defend those in power.

Struggled with self-confidence and self-esteem. You may doubt your abilities and may feel like you are not as capable as others. You may also struggle with seeking out validation and approval from others.

Felt a need to belong and to be part of a community. You may seek out groups or organizations to belong to and may feel a strong sense of loyalty and obligation to those groups. You may also struggle with feeling like an outsider or like you don't fit in.

Experienced fear or anxiety in response to perceived threats or danger. You may have a strong sense of self-preservation and may be highly attuned to potential risks and hazards. You may also struggle with managing your anxiety in response to these perceived threats.

Felt a need for security and stability. You may seek out jobs or relationships that provide a sense of security, and may be hesitant to take risks or make changes that could disrupt that stability. You may also struggle with managing your anxiety in response to potential threats to that security.

Struggled with decision-making and analysis paralysis. You may have a tendency to overthink and overanalyze situations, and may struggle with making decisions without seeking out reassurance or input from others.

Felt a strong sense of duty to protect and defend others. You may feel a strong sense of obligation to care for and protect those around you, and may struggle with setting boundaries or saying no to others.

Sixes care a lot about security and loyalty, and often seek out groups and communities to belong to. They are highly attuned to potential risks and hazards, and may struggle with managing their anxiety in response to these perceived threats. Sixes also value responsibility and duty, and may feel a strong need to protect and defend those they care about. However, they may struggle with self-doubt and seeking validation from others, leading to analysis paralysis and difficulty making decisions on their own. Overall, being a Six can be challenging, but their loyalty and dedication make them valuable members of their communities.

6W5 (Six Wing Five)

Enneagram Type 6, also known as The Loyalist, is known for their loyalty, responsibility, and strong sense of security. When a Six has a Five wing, they tend to be more introspective, analytical, and intellectual. They may have a stronger focus on knowledge and learning than other Sixes.

As a 6w5, you may find yourself constantly seeking information and knowledge to help you feel more secure and prepared for any situation that may arise. You may have a natural curiosity and desire to understand the world around you in a logical and systematic way.

The Five wing can also bring a level of detachment and independence to your personality. You may value your alone time and enjoy exploring your inner thoughts and ideas. However, this can also lead to a tendency to overthink and analyze situations, which can lead to indecisiveness and anxiety.

At times, you may struggle to balance your desire for security and stability with your need for intellectual exploration and independence. You may find yourself feeling torn between the comfort of what is familiar and the excitement of the unknown.

It is important for 6w5s to learn to trust their intuition and inner guidance, while also utilizing their intellect to make informed decisions. By finding a balance between their desire for security and their thirst for knowledge, 6w5s can achieve a sense of peace and confidence in themselves and their abilities.

As a 6w5, you may find that you excel in fields that require both practical knowledge and theoretical understanding. You may also have a natural talent for problem-solving and finding creative solutions to complex issues.

However, it is important to be aware of your tendency to overthink and second-guess yourself. Learning to trust your instincts and make decisions based on both intuition and logic can help you avoid getting stuck in analysis paralysis.

In relationships, you may find that you value deep connections and intellectual stimulation. You may prefer to take things slow and build trust gradually. It is important to find a partner who respects your need for independence and intellectual exploration, while also providing emotional support and security.

Overall, 6w5s bring a unique blend of intellectual curiosity and practical knowledge to the world. By learning to balance their desire for security and their thirst for knowledge, they can achieve a sense of inner peace and confidence in themselves and their abilities.

6w7 (Six Wing Seven)

The 6w7, or the Six with a Seven Wing, is a unique and interesting Enneagram type. As with all Enneagram types, the 6w7 has its own set of strengths and weaknesses that make it a complex and multi-dimensional personality.

The 6w7 is known for their combination of loyalty and adventurousness. They have a strong desire for security and stability, but also crave new experiences and excitement. This can create a bit of a push-pull dynamic within the 6w7's personality.

At their core, 6w7s are driven by a need for security and support. They want to feel like they can rely on someone or something when things get tough. This can make them very loyal to the people and institutions that they believe will provide that security. They are also very good at anticipating potential problems and preparing for them, which is why many 6w7s are drawn to careers in risk management or emergency services.

On the other hand, the 7 wing of the 6w7 brings a sense of curiosity and desire for adventure. 6w7s are often attracted to new experiences and are willing to take risks to try them out. They may be drawn to travel, extreme sports, or other high-intensity activities that provide an adrenaline rush. This sense of adventure can sometimes clash with the 6w7's need for security, leading to a sense of conflict within the personality.

One of the biggest challenges for the 6w7 is finding balance between these two competing desires. They want to feel safe and secure, but they also want to explore and experience new things. This can sometimes lead to a sense of restlessness or anxiety if they feel like they are not getting enough of either. They may struggle with decision-making, as they weigh the risks and benefits of each option.

Despite these challenges, the 6w7 has many strengths. They are loyal, reliable, and hardworking. They are also creative and have a knack for problem-solving. Their ability to anticipate potential problems and plan for them can make them excellent leaders and managers.

In order to thrive, the 6w7 needs to find ways to balance their need for security with their desire for adventure. They may benefit from seeking out new experiences that are also safe and structured, such as guided tours or adventure sports with experienced instructors. They can also benefit from building a strong support network of friends and family who can provide them with the security they crave.

Ultimately, the 6w7 is a complex and dynamic personality type that offers many strengths and challenges. By understanding their unique blend of loyalty and adventure, they can learn to navigate the world in a way that brings them fulfillment and happiness.

Enneagram 6's Patterns at Different Levels of Stress

As with all Enneagram types, the behavior of a Type 6 can change under stress. At different levels of stress, an Enneagram 6 may exhibit different patterns of behavior.

At low levels of stress, a Type 6 may be able to handle things well, and may even come across as confident and decisive. They may feel secure in their relationships and be able to trust their own instincts. However, as stress levels increase, their behavior may start to change.

At moderate levels of stress, an Enneagram 6 may begin to feel more anxious and fearful. They may become indecisive and struggle with self-doubt. They may seek reassurance and validation from others, and may start to question their own judgment. They may become more cautious and may start to focus more on worst-case scenarios.

At high levels of stress, an Enneagram 6 may experience a full-blown anxiety attack or panic. They may become overwhelmed and feel like they are losing control. They may start to obsess over potential threats or dangers, and may feel paranoid or suspicious of others. They may become hyper-vigilant and may struggle to relax or let their guard down.

Meet John, a hard-working employee who has been with his company for over five years. John is an Enneagram 6, and he has always been a dedicated and reliable worker. He takes pride in his work and always goes above and beyond to ensure that he meets his deadlines and produces high-quality results.

However, lately, John has been feeling more anxious and stressed than usual. His workload has increased, and he is struggling to keep up with the demands of his job. He has started to doubt his abilities and has been seeking reassurance from his colleagues and managers. He has even been second-guessing his decisions and has become more indecisive than usual.

As his stress levels continue to rise, John's behavior starts to change. He becomes more cautious and starts to focus more on the worst-case scenarios. He starts to obsess over the potential problems that may arise and starts to worry about the future of his job. He becomes hyper-vigilant and struggles to relax or let his guard down.

One day, John's anxiety reaches its peak, and he experiences a full-blown panic attack. He feels like he is losing control and starts to hyperventilate. His colleague notices that he is not feeling well and takes him to the hospital. The doctors determine that John is suffering from anxiety and recommend that he takes a break from work to focus on his mental health.

John takes this advice and decides to take a week off to focus on himself. During this time, he reflects on his behavior and starts to recognize his patterns of behavior at different levels of stress. He realizes that he has been neglecting his own needs and has been putting too much pressure on himself.

With this new awareness, John starts to take steps to manage his stress more effectively. He starts practicing deep breathing and meditation and finds that it helps him relax and clear his mind. He also starts talking to a therapist and learns healthy coping mechanisms to deal with his anxiety.

Over time, John starts to feel more in control of his emotions and behavior. He recognizes when he is starting to feel anxious and takes steps to manage his stress before it escalates. He becomes more self-aware and develops healthy coping mechanisms to navigate stressful situations.

As an Enneagram 6, John has learned that his behavior can change under stress, but with self-awareness and healthy coping mechanisms, he can manage his stress effectively and thrive in his personal and professional life.

It is important to note that these patterns of behavior are not set in stone, and that different individuals may respond differently to stress. However, understanding these patterns can be helpful in identifying when an Enneagram 6 may be experiencing stress and offering appropriate support.

If you are an Enneagram 6, it may be helpful to identify your own patterns of behavior at different levels of stress. By recognizing when you are starting to feel anxious or overwhelmed, you can take steps to manage your stress and prevent it from escalating. Some strategies that may be helpful include deep breathing, meditation, exercise, or talking to a trusted friend or therapist.

Remember, being an Enneagram 6 is not a weakness, but rather a unique way of processing the world around you. By becoming more self-aware and developing healthy coping mechanisms, you can learn to navigate stress more effectively and thrive as an Enneagram 6.

Enneagram 6: An Overview of Strengths and Blind Spots

The Enneagram is a personality system that helps individuals understand the motivation behind their behavior. It identifies nine types of personalities, each with its unique strengths and blind spots. Type 6 individuals have a need for security and safety in all aspects of their lives. They are committed, loyal, and dependable individuals who make great leaders in times of uncertainty. However, their need for security can lead to anxiety and fear, making them indecisive and hesitant in decision-making.

Strengths

Enneagram 6s are reliable and trustworthy individuals who can handle crisis situations with ease. They are always prepared for potential dangers and can foresee risks in advance. They have a strong sense of responsibility towards their commitments, making them loyal and dedicated to people, causes, and institutions. They value honesty and integrity, which makes them ideal candidates for leadership positions.

Another strength of Enneagram 6s is their cautious

and diligent nature. They are excellent at identifying potential threats and taking necessary measures to avoid them. They are meticulous in their approach, ensuring that all aspects of a project or task are thoroughly analyzed and evaluated. They are also great at anticipating problems and coming up with solutions, making them valuable members of any team.

Samantha, an Enneagram 6, had always been a reliable and trustworthy friend to those around her. She had a natural ability to handle crisis situations with ease, and her friends knew they could count on her to be there for them, no matter what. Her cautious nature meant that she was always prepared for potential dangers and could foresee risks in advance, making her an invaluable member of any group.

Samantha's strong sense of responsibility towards her commitments made her one of the most loyal and dedicated people her friends knew. Whether it was a cause she believed in, an institution she was a part of, or simply a friend who needed her support, she always gave her all. Her friends admired her honesty and integrity, which made her an ideal candidate for leadership positions.

In group projects or tasks, Samantha's diligence and attention to detail were unmatched. She would meticulously analyze every aspect and consider all potential threats, coming up with solutions before they even became problems. Her ability to anticipate issues and provide solutions made her an incredibly valuable member of any team.

All these qualities made Samantha one of the most valued and loved members of her friend group. Her reliability, dedication, and caution made her a friend that everyone knew they could count on, no matter what.

Blind Spots

One of the significant blind spots of Enneagram 6s is their excessive need for security, leading to anxiety and fear. They tend to focus too much on hypothetical worst-case scenarios, which can cause them to become overly anxious and fearful. This fear can also lead them to seek validation and reassurance from others, especially authority figures, which can make them dependent on others' opinions and decisions.

Another blind spot of Enneagram 6s is their tendency towards analysis paralysis. They tend to overthink and consider hypothetical scenarios, leading to indecisiveness and hesitation. They may get stuck in the planning phase and never take action, fearing the potential consequences of their decisions.

That sounds like a lot of mental energy, right? Let's dive into some opportunities for growth now.

Opportunities for Growth and Improvement

Enneagram 6s can improve themselves by focusing on the following areas:

Trusting Yourself

Enneagram 6s are great at looking to others for guidance and support. However, they need to learn to trust themselves more often. They must recognize that they have the knowledge, skills, and abilities to make informed decisions on their own. Cultivating a more positive inner dialogue and building self-esteem can help them trust themselves more and make decisions that are true to themselves.

Balancing Your Loyalties

Enneagram 6s value loyalty in all aspects of their life. However, they must be mindful of where they direct their loyalty. It is crucial to evaluate whether their loyalty is serving their best interests or not. Sometimes, their loyalty may lead them to remain in situations or relationships that are no longer healthy or beneficial to them. Therefore, they need to learn to balance their loyalty to others with their loyalty to themselves.

Confronting Fear

The primary motivation for security often leads to anxiety and fear for Enneagram 6s. The most significant obstacle to overcome for type 6 is to face their fear directly. They can start by identifying the root cause of their fear and then challenging it. This will help them understand that fear is not always an accurate representation of reality. By confronting their fear, they can learn to manage it better and take actions that align with their values.

Overcoming Analysis Paralysis

Enneagram 6s tend to overthink and consider hypothetical scenarios, leading to analysis paralysis and indecisiveness. To avoid this, they should try to identify the facts that are relevant to the situation and make decisions based on them. Trusting their instincts and values can also help them make decisions with greater ease. Taking action and learning to embrace mistakes as
part of the learning process can also help Enneagram 6s overcome analysis paralysis.

As mentioned, Enneagram 6s have many strengths, including their reliability, loyalty, and diligent nature. However, their excessive need for security and fear of the unknown can lead to anxiety, indecisiveness, and analysis paralysis. By focusing on trusting themselves, balancing their loyalties, confronting their fear, and overcoming analysis paralysis, Enneagram 6s can grow and improve as individuals. Understanding and embracing their strengths and blind spots can help them lead more fulfilling lives and achieve their goals.

Setting Objectives - Wheel of life Exercise.

What would you change about your life, if you could only change one thing? Better relationships: Would you choose them? a more satisfying line of work? improved health? Or perhaps you'd like to improve at something more personally meaningful, like weaving, cooking, or playing an instrument. There are so many options in your life, isn't there? Why should you pick just one, and how could you pick just one? Although you don't have to pick just one, doing so is the first step. Using a tool to gain a clearer vision will help you, regardless of whether you previously found the question to be simple to answer, required some thought, or were unable to do so.

It's possible that the area of your life where you feel the most pain is the one where you would like to make the biggest improvements. You will also have stronger values in some areas of life than others. And you'll probably perform better in those categories. We tend to gravitate towards the things we value, which makes us stronger in those areas. The Wheel of Life is one such tool; it's frequently used in coaching and examines various key life

areas, such as social, family, relationships, spirituality, career, etc. These are just suggestions; you can add whatever is significant to you.
You will need to print out a chart or create your own to complete this exercise. The good news is that a life coach I know has generously offered to send you a worksheet and a video walkthrough for the entire wheel of life process. You can do that by clicking the link below.

https://intralifestyle.com/wol-gift/

Go ahead and finish that, then come back here. If you're working alone, you should assign one of the key areas to each slice in your Wheel of Life chart. Next, you complete each one; you can grade them using a scale of 1 to 10, percentages, etc. It's crucial to have a question prepared for each section of the wheel. For instance:

How satisfied am I, on a scale of 1 to 10?
How closely am I getting to my ideal X on a scale of 1 to 10?

Try to recall your general feelings over the previous week or so as you do this. Naturally, if there have been any recent significant life events, they will almost certainly show up in your scores. By the end, you will have a visual representation of your life's potential for development. You can then start setting your goals from there. It is said that a goal that is not put in writing is just a wish.

So, are you prepared to fulfil those desires? Continue reading. Your subconscious mind needs your goals to be expressed in a way that is simple to understand. Language is how our minds "translate" the outside world. From an early age, we are taught to give words meaning. Your understanding of the world is determined by the vocabulary of your inner voice. If you choose the right words, you can change how you perceive something.

Avoid using the words "I want" when stating your goals because they are focused on what isn't there. Instead, use phrases like "I am improving at... My social life is getting better... This person's relationship with me makes me feel... Put it in the present tense as if it already exists. Since you are actually making progress in that direction and putting in the necessary effort, things are already getting better for you. The best goals are SMART - Specific, Measurable, Achievable, and Time-bound. You've probably heard this before.

Be as specific as you can, have benchmarks in mind to gauge your progress, be reasonable — change doesn't happen overnight — and set "deadlines" for each one. For instance, I'll lose one pound by the end of the month or by journaling every morning for seven days. We will discuss your potential blind spots in the most universal areas of life in the pages that follow. I am aware that not all of the areas will apply to you at this time, and some areas will take precedence. However, you can use this to gain some understanding, get around any obstacles, and come up with fresh approaches to dealing with those difficulties.

Enneagram 6 in Health and Fitness

Taking care of your physical and mental health is essential for a happy and fulfilling life. As an Enneagram 6, you may struggle with anxiety and fear, which can make it challenging to establish and stick to a health and fitness routine. However, with the right mindset and approach, you can overcome these challenges and achieve your goals. Here are some tips that can help, if they relate to you:

Start with Small Steps
Don't try to overhaul your entire lifestyle overnight. Instead, start with small, achievable goals that you can build upon over time. For example, drinking an extra glass of water per day, meditating for 2-5 minutes, going to bed 20 minutes earlier, or disconnecting from your phone for the last 30 minutes before bed.

Find a Support System
Enneagram 6s are loyal and dependable friends who thrive on the support and guidance of others. Use this to your advantage by seeking out a support system to help you on your health and fitness

journey. This could be a workout buddy, a coach or trainer, or a group of like-minded individuals. Having someone to hold you accountable and cheer you on can make a world of difference.

Get Educated

As an Enneagram 6, you may have a tendency to worry and overthink things. One way to combat this is to arm yourself with knowledge. Research different exercise programs, nutrition plans, and wellness practices to find what resonates with you. This will help you feel more confident and in control, reducing anxiety and fear.

Focus on Strengths, Not Weaknesses

Enneagram 6s can be hard on themselves and may struggle with self-doubt. Instead of fixating on your weaknesses, focus on your strengths. Maybe you're great at meal planning or love trying new workout routines. By emphasizing what you're good at, you'll build confidence and motivation, making it easier to tackle areas where you may be less comfortable.

Address Your Blind Spots

Enneagram 6s are prone to anxiety and fear, which can lead to a lack of trust in themselves and others. This can make it difficult to take risks or try new things, which can hold you back in your health and fitness journey. By acknowledging and addressing these blind spots, you can begin to overcome them. Try journaling or working with a therapist to help you identify and work through your fears.

Practice Self-Care
As an Enneagram 6, you may have a tendency to put others' needs ahead of your own. However, it's important to practice self-care to maintain your physical and mental health. This could include taking a relaxing bath, practicing meditation, or treating yourself to a massage. By prioritizing self-care, you'll be better equipped to tackle challenges and achieve your goals.

Celebrate Your Successes
Finally, make sure to celebrate your successes, no matter how small they may seem. Enneagram 6s can be hard on themselves, so it's important to acknowledge and celebrate your accomplishments along the way. Maybe you hit a new personal best on your run or stuck to your meal plan all week. Whatever it is, take a moment to celebrate and reflect on your progress.

Taking care of your health and fitness as an Enneagram 6 can be challenging, but it's not impossible. By starting with small steps, finding a support system, and focusing on your strengths, you can achieve your goals and improve your physical and mental health. Remember to address your blind spots, practice self-care, and celebrate your successes along the way. With time and dedication, you can become the healthiest version of yourself.

- Starting with small achievable goals can build confidence and momentum.
- Seek out a support system to hold you accountable and cheer you on.
- Arm yourself with knowledge to combat anxiety and fear.
- Focus on your strengths to build confidence and motivation.
- Acknowledge and address your blind spots to overcome anxiety and fear.
- Prioritize self-care to maintain physical and mental health.
- Celebrate your successes, no matter how small they may seem.

Enneagram 6 in Finances

As an Enneagram 6, your relationship with money can be complex. On one hand, you value security and stability, which may lead to a fear of financial uncertainty. On the other hand, you may feel pressure to be responsible and take care of those around you, leading to a tendency to overspend or take on too much debt. In this chapter, we will explore ways to develop a healthy relationship with finances and avoid common pitfalls for Enneagram 6 individuals.

It's important to state that it may be a superpower of yours. In fact, you may already have good spending and saving habits with a security pot of cash filled up. Especially because this is likely to be a high value of yours, having a sense of security. It's easy to see that having a high value on security and stability could lead to more stress in financial areas of life. But it may just as easily have been a driving force in order to master these skills. That being said, some of the below points may or may not be relevant for you. As usual, take what works and leave the rest.

Awareness of Spending Habits

The first step in developing a healthy relationship with money is to become aware of your spending habits. Keep track of your expenses for a week and see where your money goes. Some banking apps let you see your expenses per category. If you are overspending on takeout then you can consider alternatives but you need to know that's what you're doing, first.

Possible pitfall: One thing that is common among Enneagram 6 individuals when it comes to spending habits is a tendency to overspend on loved ones or friends. You might feel pressure to pick up the check if you hear a friend complain about their finances or make expensive gifts even if you cannot afford them.

What to do: Make a monthly budget and stick to it. Let your friends know you are doing this and you need their support. You will only go out X times this month. When you do go out/order food make sure you stick within your budget. Don't offer to split the bill for breakfast if you've had nothing but a coffee. If a friend needs to borrow money, think well before you lend it to them. You can assess your own financial situation and decide what works best for you.

Prioritizing Bills

Another common pitfall for Enneagram 6 individuals is trouble prioritizing bills. "It's okay, I'll do it later" can result in extra charges on your phone bill or, worse, you might have your electricity cut. You know the feeling; the mail arrives, and you see a bunch of letters. The Enneagram 6 in you may often say, "This can wait."

What to do: If you're not already doing it, try setting up a direct debit for your recurrent expenses and utilities. That way you'll have your bills paid and you can forget about them without getting any services cut. You only have to worry about it once and then you can forget about it for good. Many Enneagram 6 individuals report this has been a lifesaver for them. It has been advised in many financial books to set up automatic transfers for savings and bill payments.

Balancing Comfort and Growth

Enneagram 6 individuals may have a desire to make more money but often struggle with a disconnect between their very nature of seeking security and the need for growth. It can feel like a battle between comfort and growth.

Actions and desires are not aligned. When you say you want to earn more money and have a fantasy of a specific amount, it doesn't always become aligned with actions. The desire for growth and the need for comfort can cause some concerns in this area of life.

What to do: What helps here is being able to stack the benefits of earning more money and linking them to your very true essence, that is, peace. For example, how could the effort to make more money give you, even more, peace and comfort in your life? Oftentimes, you'll see what looks like an uphill battle, giving in before you've started. This can leave your fantasy to always remain just a fantasy.

Marie was an Enneagram 6 who had always struggled with her relationship with money. She was constantly worried about financial uncertainty and felt pressured to take care of her loved ones, leading her to overspend and accumulate debt.

But one day, Marie decided to take control of her finances and develop a healthy relationship with money. She started by tracking her expenses and creating a monthly budget. She let her friends know about her new approach and asked for their support in sticking to her budget.
Marie also set up direct debits for her recurrent

expenses and utilities, which helped her avoid extra charges and cut services. And instead of seeing making more money as a battle between comfort and growth, she found ways to link the two and make earning more money a source of peace and comfort in her life.

Over time, Marie's efforts paid off. She paid off her debt, saved up for a much-needed vacation, and even started investing in her future. She felt more in control of her finances and less burdened by financial worries.

One day, Marie's friend Jane approached her for a loan. Jane was struggling to make ends meet and needed help to pay her rent. Marie knew that lending money could be risky, but she also wanted to help her friend. So, she took a look at her budget and financial situation, and after careful consideration, decided to lend Jane the money.

Thanks to her new financial habits, Marie was able to help her friend without putting her own financial stability at risk. And it felt good to know that she could be there for someone in need without sacrificing her own financial wellbeing.
The moral of the story is that developing a healthy relationship with finances can bring peace and

stability to your life, and help you be there for those you care about without putting your own financial future in jeopardy.

Enneagram 6 in Relationships

Relationships are an essential part of life. Having people to care for and who care for us is important for the quality of our lives as well as our overall well-being and happiness. Many people love to have sixes in their life. Sixes are known for being loyal and dedicated to their relationships, but they can also struggle with trust and anxiety. They are constantly looking for reassurance and validation from others, which can lead to codependent relationships. As a six, you tend to worry about the future and may have a hard time letting go of the past. This can cause you to overthink situations and make decisions based on fear rather than logic. We will look at some common blind spots and areas for possible growth. Take the bits you want and leave the rest.

Blind spots and what to do:

• Fear of being alone
Sixes tend to rely heavily on their relationships for a sense of security and belonging. They fear being alone and may stay in unhealthy relationships out of fear of being single. This fear can also cause them

to hold onto grudges and past hurts, leading to resentment and mistrust. Of course, this also applies to friendships, families, and all-important relationships in life.

What to do:
Take some time to reflect on your own values and needs. It's important to know what you want out of a relationship and to be able to identify when a relationship is no longer serving you. Learn to trust your own judgment and intuition. Trust that you will be okay on your own and that you don't need someone else to make you happy. Remember that it's better to be alone than in a toxic or unfulfilling relationship.
It may be time for you to reflect on some connections and see if they are serving you well. Are you giving more than you receive? Is there a lack of boundaries? Asking yourself some important questions and reflecting will enable you to take some steps forward.

• Fear of abandonment
Sixes also fear being abandoned by their partners. This fear can cause them to be clingy and possessive, which can push their partners away. They may also have a hard time setting boundaries in their relationships, which can lead to feeling

overwhelmed and resentful.

What to do:
Learn to communicate your needs and boundaries clearly. Don't be afraid to express your feelings and concerns in a calm and rational manner. Trust that if your partner truly cares about you, they will respect your boundaries and work with you to find a compromise. Remember that setting boundaries is not selfish, it's a healthy part of any relationship.

• Overthinking
Sixes have a tendency to overthink situations and make decisions based on fear rather than logic. They may become paralyzed by their own thoughts and worry about every possible outcome.

What to do:
Practice mindfulness and focus on the present moment. Don't get caught up in the "what ifs" and "maybes" of the future. Trust that you are capable of handling whatever comes your way. Take small steps towards your goals and celebrate your accomplishments along the way. Remember that it's okay to make mistakes and that failure is a natural part of growth.

• Dependency

Sixes may become overly dependent on their partners for support and validation. This can cause them to lose sight of their own goals and aspirations.

What to do:
Take time to pursue your own interests and hobbies. Don't rely solely on your partner for happiness and fulfillment. Remember that you are a unique individual with your own strengths and talents. Pursue your own goals and dreams and encourage your partner to do the same. Support each other in your individual pursuits and come together to celebrate your accomplishments.

As a six, it's important to remember that you are capable of forming healthy and fulfilling relationships both professionally and personally. Take the time to reflect on your own needs and values, and communicate them clearly to your partner. Trust that you are capable of handling whatever comes your way and don't let fear hold you back from living your best life. Remember that relationships are a two-way street and that both partners should support and encourage each other to grow and thrive.

Enneagram 6 in Business and Career

If you are an Enneagram Type 6, you are likely loyal, responsible, and risk-averse. When it comes to your career, you may have a strong desire for job security and stability. You need to feel safe and secure in your work environment, and you want to know that you have a support system behind you.

Enneagram 6 individuals are often detail-oriented, making them great at analyzing and managing data. They are dependable and reliable, and they can be counted on to follow through on their commitments. They also have a strong sense of responsibility, which means that they are likely to take ownership of their work and go above and beyond what is expected of them.

However, Enneagram 6 individuals can also struggle with indecisiveness and self-doubt. They may have a hard time trusting themselves and their abilities, which can make it difficult for them to take risks or make bold moves in their careers.

If you are an Enneagram 6, it is important to find a

career that aligns with your values and provides a sense of security. Here are some career paths that may be a good fit for you:

Healthcare: As a Type 6, you have a natural desire to help others and provide support. Careers in healthcare, such as nursing or medical assisting, can provide a sense of purpose and security.

Law enforcement: Enneagram 6 individuals are often very responsible and rule-oriented. A career in law enforcement, such as a police officer or investigator, can provide a sense of structure and security.

Finance: Many Enneagram 6 individuals are detail-oriented and great at managing data. A career in finance, such as accounting or financial analysis, can provide a sense of stability and security.

Education: As an Enneagram 6, you have a strong sense of responsibility and a desire to help others. A career in education, such as teaching or school counseling, can provide a sense of purpose and security.

IT: Enneagram 6 individuals are often great at analyzing data and managing details. A career in IT, such as software engineering or data analysis, can provide a sense of structure and security.

However, Enneagram 6 individuals also need to be aware of their blind spots and work to overcome them in order to succeed in their careers.

Overthinking: Enneagram 6 individuals tend to overthink and worry, which can lead to indecisiveness and self-doubt. To overcome this, it is important to focus on your strengths and trust your instincts.

Avoiding risk: As a Type 6, you may be risk-averse and hesitant to take bold steps in your career. To overcome this, it is important to challenge yourself and take calculated risks.

Seeking validation: Enneagram 6 individuals may also struggle with seeking validation from others, which can lead to a lack of confidence in their own abilities. To overcome this, it is important to focus on your own goals and accomplishments, and to seek out feedback from trusted sources.

Struggling with change: Enneagram 6 individuals may also have a hard time with change and uncertainty, which can make it difficult to adapt to new situations. To overcome this, it is important to build your resilience and learn to embrace change as an opportunity for growth.

Overall, Enneagram 6 individuals have many strengths that can help them succeed in their careers. By focusing on their strengths, working to overcome their blind spots, and finding a career path that aligns with their values, they can find success and fulfillment in their work.

Enneagram 6 in Personal Development

People with Enneagram 6 personality type can find change challenging, and they may need a significant event to motivate them to want to change something in their lives. When they do make this decision, they can still resist it, so it's essential to learn how to manage this resistance. This resistance can manifest in different ways, such as procrastination or shutting down emotionally and getting trapped in old patterns. If you are an Enneagram 6 attempting to change something and fall short, it may be down to a lack of alignment. Finding ways to connect the benefits of your goals to your core values can make the process easier.

The most crucial part of an Enneagram 6's journey is discovering, embracing, and expressing the self. It's essential to start by getting to know yourself and not letting others dictate how you should live your life. Discover what makes you tick, what works for you in terms of healing, and what you want to do in any given situation.

Here are some tips to help Enneagram 6s in

personal development:

• Keep your goals to yourself.
If you are faced with an important decision or change in your life, keep it to yourself. It can be tempting to share your thoughts and get advice from others, but their views may not serve you. Spending time with your emotions and thoughts can help you find the direction you need. If something doesn't feel right, listen to your internal world and ask questions like, "What does this feeling mean?" or "Have I experienced this before?" Be curious and learn to listen to your inner compass.

• Avoid getting sidetracked.
Enneagram 6s may struggle with getting sidetracked by various voices or vices, which can lead to numbing their feelings. It's important to practice moderation and not overdo anything. Start small and commit to one small change at a time. It's unrealistic to expect significant changes overnight, so it's best to begin with SMART (Specific, Measurable, Achievable, Realistic, Time-Orientated) objectives. For example, start with journaling or words of affirmation for 21 days and then add 10 minutes of meditation.

• Give yourself time to reflect.
With so much noise and chaos, it's easy to slip into an automated way of living, full of distractions. Self-reflection is crucial, and learning how to put yourself in a "meta" position and see yourself as you repeat certain patterns can be helpful. Becoming aware of your patterns is key to the healing process. Take time to unlearn what you need and gain new tools to help you move forward. Journaling can be a helpful tool to keep track of your feelings and emotions.

Remember that personal development is a journey, and it's okay to take your time. Committing to small changes and staying focused on your goals will help you make progress towards a more fulfilling life. The fact that you're reading this book shows you have curiosity and a desire to develop yourself further, so props to you.

Conclusion

Dear Six,

You've travelled this far in search of advice on how to find the peace you've been yearning for. An uncertain future can be frightening, especially if you've spent years putting it off. But keep in mind to move slowly, be kind to yourself, and recognise your strengths because they will serve as your engines for change.

Let's start by determining the areas of your life that you want to enhance as you embark on your journey. To assist you in this, use the Wheel of Life. To get started, you can view a video walkthrough and download a free worksheet. Take your time and consider each point carefully... Ask yourself, "What do I want?" and jot down the first thing that comes to mind. Repeat this exercise for each slice of the wheel, and once you have a few lines for each, start setting your objectives.

Be aware of any potential blind spots as you work to accomplish your goals. Use the advice given to assist you in avoiding setbacks. If you make a mistake, be kind to yourself and keep going.

Pay attention to your body's needs for improved health and fitness. Eat when you're hungry, take a nap when you're tired, and make time for enjoyable activities. Be patient; results take time to appear. Learn to put your own needs and priorities first when it comes to money. If it doesn't benefit you, you don't have to spend money on others.

Practice being genuine and establishing boundaries in your relationships. Keep in mind that saying "no" is acceptable and doesn't make you a bad person.

Use your resources wisely and speak up when you disagree for a more fulfilling career. Wait until you've finished your own work before assisting others. Last but not least, be sure to schedule time for personal growth.
Be aware of your actions and pass judgement with kindness. Keep in mind that acceptance, not resistance, is the source of change. You'll discover that accepting yourself without criticism makes it simpler to accept change and proceed.

Remember that you're capable of achieving anything you set your mind to. Believe in yourself, and you'll find the peace you've been seeking.

You've got this.